PERFECT CHRISTIAN DIVINE WAY

Rules and Regulations for Members

As a social member it does not devolve upon you to make contributions to the Cause unless you so desire. You may show your appreciation in whatever manner you see fit. We leave it to your judgment to do what you believe is right - for you will always do the right thing at the right time. THIS IS THE LAW.

We make it incumbent upon you to report to us at least once a week, either in person or by message. This is to keep you in touch with the vibrations effecting our cult, and for your protection.

Should you be fitted to become a teacher and desire to become qualified for such work, you will be placed in the hands of a master teacher, who will lead you into the necessary wisdom. See our Master Teacher.

W. E. Riker

PUBLICATIONS

BETTY LEWIS

○○○○○○○○○○

1974 - Victorian Homes of Watsonville
Pajaro Valley Historical Association
Revised Edition 1981

1975 - Walking & Driving Tour of Historic Watsonville
(Pamphlet) Sponsored by Chamber of Commerce,
Watsonville Main Street, Pajaro Valley Historical Assc.
10th printing - 1992

1975 - Highlights in the History of Watsonville
Watsonville Federal Savings & Loan for their
50th Anniversary

1976 - Watsonville: Memories That Linger
Otter B Books, Santa Cruz
3rd Printing - 1986

1977 - Monterey Bay Yesterday
Otter B Books, Santa Cruz
2nd Printing - 1987

1978 - Watsonville Yesterday
Mehl's Colonial Chapel - 100 radio programs

1980 - Watsonville: Memories That Linger Vol. II
Western Tanager Press, Santa Cruz

1985 - W. H. Weeks, Architect
Pioneer Publishing Co., Fresno
Revised Edition - 1989

1992 - Holy City: Riker's Roadside Attraction
Otter B Books, Santa Cruz

HOLY CITY

RIKER'S ROADSIDE
ATTRACTION

IN THE SANTA CRUZ MOUNTAINS

HOLY CITY

RIKER'S ROADSIDE
ATTRACTION

IN THE SANTA CRUZ MOUNTAINS

A NOSTALGIC HISTORY
BY
BETTY LEWIS

OTTER B BOOKS
Santa Cruz, California
1992

HOLY CITY: Riker's Roadside Attraction

TOPICS IN MONTEREY BAY AREA HISTORY

Published by Otter B Books
December, 1992

ISBN 0-9617681-5-0

Made in the United States of America.
Graphic design by Lizardgraphics, Santa Cruz.

The author and publisher reiterate that we are reporting some of
Riker's ridiculous if not abhorent racist ravings as illustration of his
incoherent philosophy and the political atmosphere of the time,
with our hope that we never be condemned to repeat it.

TABLE OF CONTENTS

This book is dedicated to the Sourisseau Academy, History Department, San Jose State University, for the enthusiastic and continued support of my research projects over the last nineteen years by way of ten research grants.

-Betty Lewis

FOREWORD

Anyone who ever traveled the old San Jose - Santa Cruz highway in the '20's, '30's and '40's will well remember Holy City with all its garish signs, Santa Claus statues and penny peep shows. Betty Lewis, noted Watsonville historian, has spent several years researching Holy City and "Father" Riker, founder of this so-called "religious" cult. She has done this by way of a research grant from the Sourisseau Academy, San Jose State University, who have said; "The fact that you have received more grants from the academy than any other individual attests to the fine quality of your research and your enthusiasm for local history. The Board of Trustees of the Sourisseau Academy counts it a privilege to be able to support your research."

This is Mrs. Lewis' sixth historical book; she writes articles about the history of the Pajaro Valley for the *Register Pajaronian.* and uses many of her 30,000 collection of post cards to illustrate her publications. She grew up in Santa Cruz and married Monte Lewis of Watsonville. They have four children and seven grandchildren. She was named Watsonville's Woman of the Year for 1986 and has received numerous awards for her research and writing. Her dedicated and avid interest in the area's history has led to its preservation for the present generation and those to follow.

(signed - Henry J. Mello)
California State Senator

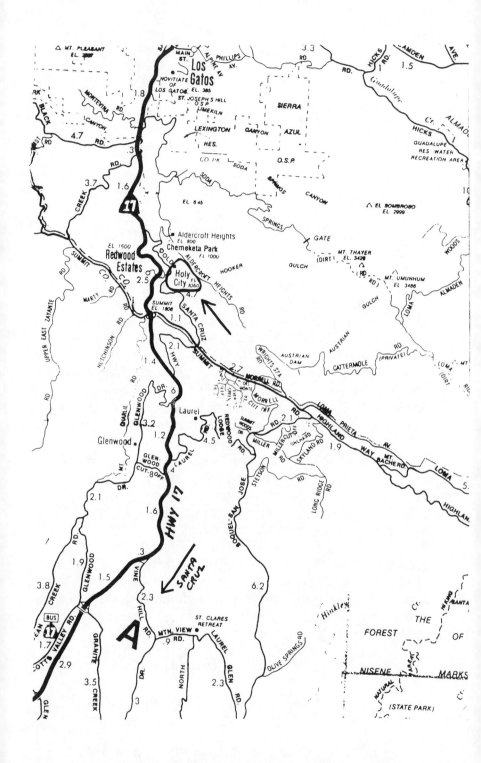

INTRODUCTION

When I was growing up in Santa Cruz, California, in the 1930's, our car route from home to San Jose, or other northern points, was by way of the old, two-lane road that passed through Holy City south of Los Gatos. My very conservative, Presbyterian-Elder father did not look favorably upon this carnival type village. My older brother, Bob, and I were absolutely fascinated - especially with the Santa Claus statues that stood all in a row welcoming the many tourists that passed through this strange place. I don't even remember the name of "Father" Riker being mentioned and it probably wouldn't have meant a thing to me, anyway, at that age.

For younger travellers, a whole row of Santas at Holy City was irresistable.

When I started my post card collection some twenty years ago, I remembered Holy City and those statues. I was determined to find some Holy City cards and it was not easy. The first one was given to me by a friend and fellow collector, the late Sam Stark of Pebble Beach. It showed a two-lane, curving road winding through the trees. On the face of the card it said, "Road to Holy City," and that brought back another memory - car sickness!

I soon alerted fellow deltiologists and dealers of my wish to find more of these post cards. Believe me, they are not only hard to find but can be very expensive. A black and white real photo card of Holy City can cost up to $35 or $40, though I've been able to buy a few at lesser prices.

Someone mentioned that a doctor at U.C. Davis had a number of Holy City post cards in mint condition. I had met Carroll Cross and talked to him several times about our mutual hobby. I dropped him a line inquiring if I could see these particular cards. He very kindly stopped by my office one day bringing seventeen fanastic views of Holy City. He had been to a flea market in Sacramento and purchased an old album of post cards, of which the only decent ones were those of Holy City. He left them with me to copy for use in this book. I guarded them with my life until I could return them several months later.

Dr. Cross is one of many who have helped with my research, and I have indeed been fortunate to have met so many informative and helpful people. Researching Holy City for the past few years has been an exciting and rewarding experience. My only wish would be to go back to a day in the 1930's and once again see Holy City as it was - to a youngster's eye it was an exciting and mysterious place.

Betty Bagby Lewis

HOLY CITY

RIKER'S ROADSIDE
ATTRACTION

IN THE SANTA CRUZ MOUNTAINS

FATHER RIKER, THE WISE MAN OF THE FAR WEST

'I came into this world to introduce a *NEW WORLD* within our present world. It will be a new world of *Supreme Law and Order*, harmoniously working. It is also known as the Jew and Gentile *NEW WORLD*.'   -'*Father*' *Riker*

Typical polemical card put out by Holy City Press, 1940's.

CHAPTER I

RIKER & EVANGELISM

One of the greatest promoters of all times was William Edward Riker who never let pass an opportunity for theatrics, preaching or just plain bamboozaling the public to his way of thinking. Considering today's world of religious madmen, media crackpots, extremist cults, Riker was an earlier, comparatively little known fanatic who described himself as "The Emancipator". He claimed that California "Is a white man's home" and declared that he had the solution for the "World's Perfect Government". He founded Holy City in the Santa Cruz mountains in 1919 under the doctrine of the "Perfect Christian Divine Science". Some wag said he "must have named it that because it was neither Christian, divine nor scientific, and if improved what could it have been originally?"

There were other "religious" leaders around at that time such as George Baker who, also in 1919, founded the Peace Mission Movement and took on the name of Father Divine. Based in New York and Philadelphia, the movement attracted thousands on the principals of renunciation of personal property, communal living,

Postcards showing approaches to Holy City, with its ubiquitous signs.

celibacy, and bans on liquor, tobacco, cosmetics and movies. Unlike Riker, he preached racial equality and the members were mostly black. Each "settlement" was called "heaven," where informal religious services were held. The movement came to a quick halt after Father Divine's death on September 10, 1965, when he was in his late 80's.

Also of the same period was Aimee Semple McPherson, born in 1890, who settled in Los Angeles in 1918. She had many followers of her preaching and healing movement which was called the International Church of the Four Square Gospel (her vision of heaven with four walls). She wrote a number of books and raised monies to build the Angelus Temple in Los Angeles. (some say that Riker donated $10,000 to her cause). Her sermons at this huge ediface were broadcast over the radio station she owned. Thousands of worshippers attended her razzle-dazzle services. She died in Oakland, California on September 27, 1944.

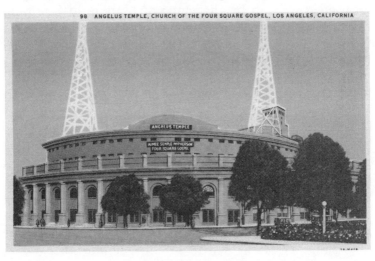

98 ANGELUS TEMPLE, CHURCH OF THE FOUR SQUARE GOSPEL, LOS ANGELES, CALIFORNIA

Evangelism was big business in the 1920's and 30's.

Riker, compared to his contemporaries, was a small fish in a big pond, though he attracted attention wherever he went and whatever he did. Born on February 17, 1873 in Oakdale, California, his family soon moved to Oroville where he abandoned school while in the fourth grade. His father died when William was 17 and the young boy became head of a household which consisted of his three sisters, a brother and his mother. Two years later his mother remarried and Riker left for greener pastures in San Francisco, where he was to hold down a number of various jobs. He also became fascinated with spiritualism and began delving into mystical and religious subjects. Soon he was preaching his "divine" message on street corners and in assembly halls - everywhere and anywhere that people would listen to him. Many did, especially women who were drawn to this young and good looking messiah.

Riker moved up and down the West Coast and married a woman by the name of Marene in Colorado Springs. While still married to her he married Bessie Zetty in December of 1907 and a son - Francois Villon Riker - was born of this union in Oakland on September 15, 1909. From the *San Francisco Chronicle*, January 6, 1909: "Fearing the abduction of her four-month-old child at the hands of the father who deceived her, she alleges by marrying her without obtaining a legal separation from his first wife, Mrs. Bessie Zetta Riker, living in seclusion in this city (Oakland) has appealed to the police for protection against W. E. Riker, a so-called divine healer, who is believed to be in Redding, Shasta County...It is said that Riker fled this city when he learned that his first wife, Mrs. M. Riker, was living at the Globe Hotel at Thirteenth Street and Broadway. Before going, however, he threatened to return to take possession of his child." In 1910 he was again with his wife, Bessie, in Texas but she up and left him and her son deciding an associate of Riker's was a better bet!

In 1914, Riker married Lucille Jensen, later to be known as "Mother" Riker, in Omaha, Nebraska. It's unclear from the records if or when he divorced his first wives. In 1915, while traveling to the East Coast and back again preaching his new religion - "The Perfect Christian Divine Science", Riker gathered together eleven disciples who lived at 674 Hayes Street in San Francisco. One of these was Stephen Rozum who had heard Riker on a street corner in Pueblo, Colorado and had followed him to San Francisco and on, eventually, to Holy City.

From Wes Peyton's "San Jose: A Personal View" Lou Murphy recalls - "I knew Stephen 'Rosie' Rozum best. He was a former Hindu monk who trained for Catholic priesthood in Poland and joined Riker in 1916. He was in his 60s in 1953. A slim, energetic man, he had the only new car in Holy City and the most profitable business in town, the Holy City Print Shop. His shop was spacious and well-equipped, and in exchange for free rent and the use of his equipment to print the Mountain Echo, we helped him hand-set ads from the California job case, run off business cards on the job press and swept the shop...." The Mountain Echo was published by Lou Murphy and Charles Norman between 1953 and 1955

At the headquarter's for the "Divine Way" in the 600 block of Hayes Street in San Francisco, such businesses as a cobbler's shop, transfer and storage company, printer's shop and general store were thriving and supporting Riker's quest for becoming the "great Emancipator". Monies were being set aside into the acquisition of the future Holy City in the Santa Cruz mountains where Riker had visited earlier. This fund was augmented by donations from the disciples and the

sale of property owned by a member named Frieda
Schwartz.

In September of 1918, William Riker, I.B. (Irwin)
Fisher and Anna Schramm, secretary, filed official
Articles of Incorporation for *The Perfect Christian
Divine Way* in Los Angeles. Between 1914 and 1919
PCDW was divided between Los Angeles and San
Francisco. At Fisher's suggestion, "Science" had been
changed to "Way". This same year, Mrs. Rosa Haas of
662 Hayes Street in San Francisco, complained that the
buzz-saw used by the colony whined day and night.
When the Judge, at the hearing, asked Riker "Isn't it
your principal to do unto others as you would have
them do unto you?" "No," said Riker, "Our faith is
founded on this principle, mind your own business."
Mother Riker brought forward the saw all wrapped up
and the Judge dismissed the case on the understanding
that the saw would be kept in that condition.

CHAPTER II

HOLY CITY IN THE SANTA CRUZ MOUNTAINS

"Father" Riker and "Mother" Lucille purchased land south of Los Gatos from Julia and Cyrus Hoult consisting of 30.25 acres for the sum of $10 in July of 1919. This land bordered on the old San Jose-Santa Cruz road and was soon to be dubbed Holy City by "Father" Riker.

Holy City, California

A road winds round where trails lead down,
To a niche in the mountains where -
The redwoods rear their lofty heads
'Neath skies that are mellow and fair.

A forest of pines on the mountain side,
Where deer with their fawns run through
And chipmunks play on a mammoth log
Is a scene of the wild I view.

A babbling brook plays down between,
The hillsides fringed with pine;
And sings its song so merrily
That I found the place divine.

The sough of the wind in the forest there,
Like stories in childhood rhymes,
Tells something of love and a tenderness
In song of those whispering pines.

When shadows grow dim at twilight hour
There's a hush in the life it knows
For silence reigns where the forest lies
Enwrapped in a kind repose.

- Lyman B. Parks (no date)

Home of Father and Mother Riker.
Holy City, Calif.

Riker's drayage business was soon hard at work dragging materials from the San Francisco area to Holy City; much of the materials were left over from the 1906 earthquake and the Panama Pacific Exposition. The disciples moved into small, roughly built shacks while the Rikers settled into a two-story house atop a knoll above the newly formed "religious cult" community. Now about thirty strong, the inhabitants were separated from their spouses (what few there were) and, needless to say, no children were ever born at Holy City! At this "New Jerusalem", disciples turned over all their wordly possessions to "Father" Riker who proclaimed that his new kingdom was being built right over the other Jerusalem on the other side of the world.

Shack that typified the housing facilities for the "disciples".

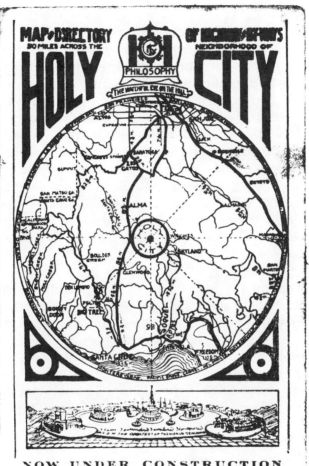

MAP & DIRECTORY
30 MILES ACROSS THE
OF RICHNESS/RIKER'S
NEIGHBORHOOD OF

HOLY CITY

PHILOSOPHY

THE WATCHFUL EYE ON THE MALL

NOW UNDER CONSTRUCTION

BY THE HOLY CITY ORGANIZATION, FOR THE PURPOSE
OF DEMONSTRATING THE IDEAL CHRISTIANITY,
DRAMA, BUSINESS SUCCESS AND POLITICS.

(OVER)

Rikercentric map on cover of pamphlet promoting the new city.

A small pamphlet, published by Riker and not dated, stated the following: "Now Under Construction - By the Holy City organization, for the purpose of demonstrating the ideal christianity, drama, business success and politics. The founders of the Holy City are the wisest of all wise men. A $10,000 challenge to the whole world who wishes to debate upon the subject of politics or religion and win the debate...Be sure and stop at the Holy City for the good eats at city prices. Free up-to-date large size rest rooms. Service, accommodations, greatest of courtesy is our motto." Riker's philosophy was that the white man and the Jewish race were supreme while the negro and orientals were the inferior races.

Also in the pamphlet - "List of various businesses that the Holy City is engaged in: Fully equipped Garage, Super Service Station, Restaurant and Soda Stands, Auditorium, Dance Ballroom, Lecture Hall, Motion Pictures, Notary Public, Visit Holy City Zoo, Grocery Store, General Store, Butcher Shop, Home Bakery, Barber Shop, Shoe Repair Shop, Public Stenographer, Printing Shop, Free 18 seat Public Comfort Stations and radio station KFQU - our Perfect Service is Always At Your Disposal." Over the doorway to the dance hall was a sign that proclaimed: "Agreeable dancing is as near heaven as any mortal will ever get."

The businesses and attractions at the center of Holy City.

Main road from the other direction, with the Press on the far right.

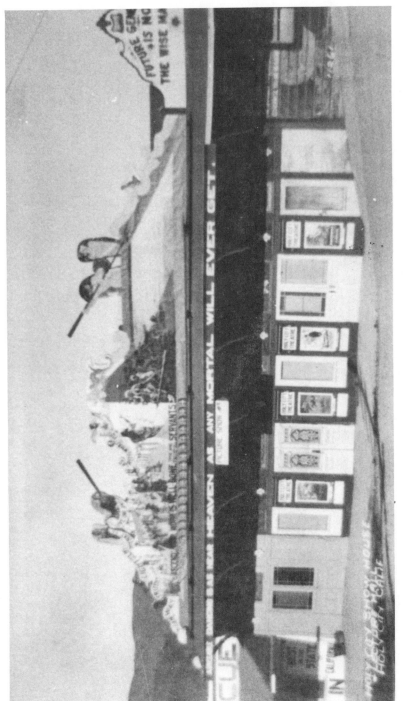

Garish signs on "Showhouse & Lecture Hall."

During the 20's the Watsonville Cowboy Wranglers, a small group of musicians, appeared on radio station KFQU. The leader was a man by the name of Smitty according to Shirley Bagby Sharon of Salinas, whose father, Samuel LeRoy Bagby, had been a member of the group. In December of 1931, station KFQU was shut down by the Federal Radio Commission saying "The commission held the station was not operated in the public interest and had frequently deviated from its assigned frequency." This "deviation" infuriated nearby residents who had no interest in Riker's ramblings! KFQU had been licensed in 1924; 1,420 kilocycles, 100 watts.

back row left: ?, Henry Rogers, Samuel LeRoy Bagby, ?;
front: Chet Handley and Smitty, leader of the Wranglers.

Holy City radio station KFQU.

CHAPTER III

PROBLEMS, PAMPHLETS, PACKARDS

"Father" Riker was always in and out of trouble with the law - but never convicted. From the *San Francisco Chronicle,* October 18, 1921: "For more than three years the cult has been the object of investigation by the police, the state board of charities and corrections and the department of justice, but the nature of the complaints has until the present time left the investigators handicapped in taking any legal action against its practices."

In November of that same year, also in the *Chronicle,* "William E. Riker and his wife, Lucille, head of the Perfect Christian Divine Way, a religious cult, who were recently indicted by the grand jury on charges of obtaining money under false prestenses and conspiring to corrupt public morals, were yesterday sued for $100,000 damages by Alexander Schwartz, a former member of the cult." This suit carried on until June of 1923 when Anna Schwartz died. Her eldest son, Fred, took the witness stand and declared "that many of the allegations set forth in the complaint against the Rikers were not true." Superior Judge Roache dismissed the charges - case closed.

"Father" William & "Mother" Lucille in later years.

Mrs. Evelyn Rosencrantz of Los Angeles sued Riker
in a breach of promise suit in 1928, claiming he had
lived with her in Palm City for two months and had
promised to marry her. Mrs. Rosencrantz had been at
San Quentin for several "stretches" on bad check
charges. "San Francisco police records show that the
woman (Rosencrantz) has been known as Mrs. P.E. Reid,
Evelyn Barton, Mrs. Van Dohen, Ella Barton and Lizzie
Barton. She was first received at San Quentin on
December 8, 1915 from Oakland on a bad check charge.
She was released January 18, 1918, a record which does
not compare with the war-time information. She was
also held as a parole violator. Her next term started on
May 28, 1919, from San Diego for bad checks. She was
released on January 6, 1920, on a court order granting her
a new trial. She was held to answer on January 9, 1923
and sentenced to San Quentin where she stayed for
more than four years." *San Francisco Chronicle,* January
4, 1923

"You know Riker met Mrs. Rosencrantz last
October at a radio meeting here (Los Angeles). She is a
very unusual woman and immediately attracted his
attention. She told him she had been forced to serve a
term in prison for forgery to save her 21 year-old son
and he believed her." - Irwin Fisher, *San Francisco
Chronicle* January 2, 1928

Rosencrantz claimed that "Father" Riker had given
her a book entitled *Diamond Key Book* which included
the ten commandments for women, according to
Riker's philosophy, and that he had tried to get it away
from her on numerous occasions without success.

Commandment #1 - *'Marry for a bank account or any other account should it be your choice. If man would demonstrate more freedom with his pocketbook, woman would not be tempted to marry for money.'*

#2 - *'Either after or before marriage thou shalt do all things your soul intelligence directs you to do, and tell your husband to do likewise.'*

#3 - *'Thou shalt acknowledge fashion to your own advantage, enjoyment and satisfaction in this particular age, until you no longer have reason to. For, should woman cease to do something to cause men to take an interest in her (since he is duty bound to do so) he would soon become dormant, inactive so to speak.'*

#4 - *'Thou shall talk and gossip all you wish over man's weaknesses, but make it your religion not to find fault with your own sex, for they are doing the same thing that you are doing, trying to entertain and awaken man.'*

#5 - *'Thou shall not be envious over thy sister who has good luck, for you have the same power within you if you will but use it to inspire some man who has plenty, and if he has not, to go and get it so that he may supply you with the so-called luxuries of life.'*

#6 - *'Thou shall not choose a condemning minister to be thy guide or thy God. You have your own Soul Divine Self, which is one with God, to guide you.'*

#7 - *'Thou shall not neglect they husband's child while it be in thy possession, but when thou hast delivered it into this world and to him, command him to employ the servant that God gave to the white man to care for it.'*

#8 - 'Thou shall love God and his laws with all thy heart, then love the good that the man you call yours does for you and love him last until he fails you. When man proves he has the power to protect you from all poverty and sorrow (a man like Jesus Christ) it is then time enough for him to demand first love instead of last.'

#9 - 'Thou shall see all places and things Godlike and this will keep you Godly, inspired, happy, healthy, harmonious and successful.'

#10 - 'Thou shall not misplace the bible so in case the minister calls, thou mayest ask him various questions concerning its contents and compel him to prove his arguments and non-contradictions, logic and works; ask him also if he has removed the beam from his own eyes.'

Rosencrantz also charged that Riker had promised to star her in a movie to be entitled "The Perfect Woman" and afterwards she was to fly from Holy City to Rome in a plane designed like the *Spirit of St. Louis* and named *Spirit of Love*. Riker had a movie studio built at Holy City; speculating that since a movie had been made in the area he would soon reap the benfits of any future movies. The building was never used for its intended purpose and eventually served as a dormitory.

Riker denied all charges and in June of 1928, Rosencrantz was sentenced again to San Quentin prison for life without parole, on her fourth conviction of bad check passing under the habitual criminal law. This life sentence precluded prosecution of Riker and the whole affair died down except in subsequent newspaper articles when reporters dug it up again.

Riker liked big, black cars, mostly Cadillacs, drove them rather recklessly, to say the least. He was fined several times for speeding and was involved in a number of accidents. He ran down two pedestrians at Mission Street and Ocean Avenue in San Francisco on September 26, 1928. According to the newspapers at that time both men suffered broken legs and internal injuries. In October of 1929, he was charged with driving on the wrong side of the road in San Mateo at 40 miles an hour in a 20 mile an hour speed zone. He paid the $10 fine but "before the clerk had the greenback tucked away the King of Holy City launched into a fervent sermon on his 'religious teachings.'" Religion had nothing to do with his philosophy, which was strange, disjointed and very peculiar. Riker also told a reporter at this time that "I had a son, but thank God, I got rid of him."

William Balch, a former Los Gatos banker, tells of

Riker driving up to the bank in his red, white and blue
painted Cadillac accompanied by his dog, a fox terrier,
who would wait in the car while his master was doing
his banking. Riker brought in all cash and had yellow
checks made up with a picture of Jesus on one corner.
He would sit and talk, and talk, boring anyone within
earshot with his ramblings and "divine" thoughts.
When his dog got tired of waiting in the car, he would
put his paw up on the horn and blast away until Riker
came out of the bank.

Balch recalls that "My brother (Carl) brought a
monkey home. We had it for about nine months. He
would sit on your lap and sleep then wake up and start
to bite. He bit my brother very badly one time so we
gave him away to some man but the monkey shook all
the apples out of his apple tree so he gave the monkey
to the Holy City Zoo. I never saw the monkey after that
but he was up there. He name was "Morocco"; not a
South American monkey as he couldn't hang by his
tail."

In the 1920's, Carl was a State Traffic Officer assigned
to the Santa Cruz Highway from Los Gatos to the
County line at the summit. "I do not recall when, or
where, I saw the first car, truck or pickup go by with the
initials PCDW. Over a period of time, repeated sightings
raised questions as to where the vehicles came from and
what the initials meant. I finally found out this was the
Perfect Christian Divine Way and was the name of a
religious group in the Santa Cruz mountains, this then
became Holy City...Riding the highway we more or less
made Holy City our headquarters. The group was most
accomodating as they should have been. They were the
only garage on the road and vapor locks, over-heated
engines, wrecks to be removed from the highway; they
were the ones who benefited. I must say they must have
been reasonably honest and fair as I never heard a

Before Highway 17 was built, the "garage service" was very busy.

customer complain which certainly differed from today's conditions."

William Sheehy, of San Jose, recalls seeing Riker park his white packard in front of the San Jose post office and go about getting recruits to join his sect in Holy City and join his "happy Kingdom". Riker also drove around town using a loud speaker to spout out his own brand of philosophy; it was hard to miss the car with all of the signs upon it and the bright colors assaulting your eyes!

> In heart and mind - in purpose,
>   On this rock that's firm and dry
> They are building a New City
>   For the Godlike and Most High,
> Where they'll dwell in peace and comfort,
>   From the serpents face away;
> This cult, so-called, now landed,
>   Is the Perfect Christian Way.
>
> - Mother Lucille Riker
> from New World Utopias by Paul Kagan

According to Willie Frank, who has lived near Holy City since 1918, Joe Albert was carrying some money while walking through Holy City when he was shot several times; robbed and left for dead, he later recovered. The assailant was never caught nor was the money ever found.

During the depression, it was said that 42,000 meals were served to transients at Holy City - "an hour's work for a square meal." Riker held Sunday morning services in the Redwood Grove - more philosophical than religious. In the Riker's home, on one wall, there were pictures of Mother Lucille, Marilyn Monroe, George Washington, Adolph Hitler and Abraham Lincoln - quite a diverse collection!

The soda works was quite successful, especially during Prohibition. According to one source, *Hawaiian Punch* was developed in Holy City and the recipe later sold. Ginger Ale and *Golden Glow* beer were also produced along with *Fruit Bowl* and *3 in One*. 15 cents bought a drink at the bar and if a customer bought three, the bartender would buy the next one.

Main road curves in front of bottling works.

Some of the disciples names connected with Holy City over the years were: Joe Albert, butcher and manager at Holy City; Miss Winifred Allington, postmistress; Otto R. Bodinger, ex-German soldier; Elsie Burch; Jim Edmondson, gas station operator; Agnes Jenkins, Arthur Kastner, zoo keeper; Arthur Landstrum, clerk; Charles Lott; George S. Nixon; Emil Reichsteiner, barber shop; Stephen Zygmond Rozum, printer; Fred Rommel, electrician; Earl Russell, custodian; Anna Schramm; Alexander Schwartz; Frieda Schwartz; Gotlieb Strauss, Emma Strauss, (his wife) and their daughter, Marguerite; Charlie Northy, Joseph Witzig, observatory; Irwin "Crazy" Fisher, mechanic whom Riker met in Minnesota.

In its heyday, Holy City was a fascinating stop for travelers on the old road between Santa Cruz and San Jose. They were confronted with signs, placards, loud music and Riker himself preaching his "perfect" philosophy to anyone who would listen - or, even if they didn't listen. You could eat, drink, gas your car or look at the penny peep shows which were housed in miniature steepled churches and offered "temptations" such as the crudely made legs of "Queen Elizabeth of Egypt".

One of the placards announced that you could "Look into the mirror and for sure you will see God dreaming." Many old timers remember the row of nine wooden Santa Claus statues on top of a low brick wall. There was a fountain in the middle called "The Fountain of Health" with a sign saying "This water for sick people only." At one time, Riker was going to build a "stairway to the stars" near the observatory but it was never completed. There were two 14 inch telescopes and you could look at the moon or stars for 25 cents. On May 4, 1927 a post office opened in Holy City with Father Riker as the first postmaster and this was a favorite

A line of placards and penny peep shows in miniature churches to attract your attention.

place for mail around Christmas time with the Holy City postmark being most timely. This post office closed down in 1986.

Judge John Ball of San Jose grew up in Chemaketa Park, near Holy City, and recalls that he and his family would use the services at Riker's "kingdom," such as: shoe repair, gas station, groceries, etc., and also view the astrological exhibits at the observatory.

Santas plus a woman statue used on floats used in "propaganda parades."

Sign for the zoo above the observatory. Captions flanking the observatory read, "The Law that governs the Solar System is Christianity. In the True Light Holy City reveals the Mystery" and "Two Giant Telescopes Open for Visitors Every Night."

If astronomy was good, lunar real estate should be, too.

The following is from one of Riker's many pamphlets: "Holy City in God's Country, California, the spiritual melting pot of U.S. Don't forget that this Holy City is the only Holy City that ever was on earth. The contents of this leaflet is just a sample. Please read carefully several times. This ideal Holy City demonstrates and gives the best of everything. Best interpretation, good will and love for mankind, People and Self Government, Enviornment, Scenery and Climate, Association, Philosophy and new drama, Spirituality and spirit, Service, Quality, etc. Father Riker says: If you can't be a wise man, then throw away your dogmatic churchianity and just be a human-being good fellow and then you will be a credit to common sense, Brotherhood and Christianity. Don't forget that in this age religious division is a criminal curse..."

CHAPTER IV

HEYDAY

Holy City, in 1929, was contacted by the Internal Revenue. They had decided that the "kingdom" was no longer exempt as a religious enity as there were no voluntary monetary contributions; it was a business. This same year Riker decided to hire a promoter of carnivals and revivals to set something up for Holy City along these lines. When the man, by the name of Pete, heard his crazy ideas he decided to tell the *San Francisco Examiner* and they set up a meeting in a San Francisco hotel room whereby Riker and two con men (newspaper reporters) would talk over the scheme. In the next room, listening in and taking notes, were a stenographer, physician and a judge.

Riker talked of an ampitheatre seating 17,000 people; bodies lifted up to heaven by wires and mirrors; men from the colony to masquerade as crippled, blind and deaf then to be magically cured by the "Father." He told them "there are three kinds of people - those with dough, the intelligent ones and those without dough." Naturally, all the people who came to see these marvels would pay and the good "Father" would reap the monetary benefits. "My people will do anything I tell them to do. To them I am God." One of the reporters came to Holy City under the pretense of mapping out a

"Holy City Airport"

Joe Witzig claimed that "Riker spent $15,000 alone on steam shovel work to make the airplane landing field."

big theatre and other would-be attractions thought up by
Riker.

"For a week this Examiner reporter lived as a
member of the Holy City colony. He tramped up and
down the hills and ravines of the 100 acre 'kingdom'
sketching, driving stakes with the aid of the divine
carpenter-astrologer, Joe Witzig, dragging a 50 foot
measuring tape, making estimates of lumber and
writing reams of publicity at night. The publicity, of
which the following is a sample, bore the enthusiastic
approval of 'Father' Riker and was to be released to the
newspapers of the Nation when the stage had been set
and the preliminary 'come on' propaganda had
appeared: 'All eyes are turned upon Holy City, that
Mecca of Miracles that nestles in the Santa Cruz
mountains, midway between San Francisco and the
historic shores of Monterey Bay. Visitors, sight-seers
and disciples are thronging the roadways from all
sections of the Middle West and, in fact, even the far
East. From Seattle on the north to San Diego on the
south, the west coast is aroused over the reports of
unusual healings that have already been made in his
terrestrial paradise of the Pacific.'" - *San Francisco
Examiner*, January 24, 1929

When all this deception came out into the open,
through many, many articles in the San Francisco
newspapers, Riker denied all of it saying he had known
all along what was going on. His grandiose scheme
came to naught but gathered a lot of publicity which
brought even more people to Holy City. The
"emancipator" laughed all the way to the bank!

In the *San Francisco Examiner*, January 25, 1929. was
a picture of Marguerite Strauss, 15 years old along with
the following information: "Servant of 'The King'-

Marguerite Strauss was separated from her parents at Holy City and forced to live in seclusion at Riker's sanctum where she performed menial tasks." Nothing ever came of these startling charges.

The many pamphlets spewed out from the printing press were available for a small price, including "The Final Wisdom and Understanding For You." Included in this was the pronouncement that "Mortal woman is man's only legitimate enemy, and mortal man is her only legitimate undeveloped child. In the end, when developed, both will be human beings at peace, and not arguing men and women." In 1932, Riker published a book titled "Womankind Is God In the Flesh." Other booklets by Riker included: "The Cause of Infantile Paralysis Explained," 14 pages; "The Perfect System of Government"; "The Great Eye Opener"; "The Master Mind Discipleship Book"; "The Great Jewish People"; "The Whole Truth and Nothing But the Truth" and the "Book of Books That Surely Sizzles With the Final Wisdom of God."

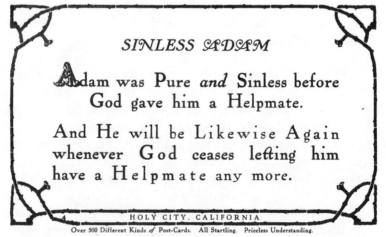

SINLESS ADAM

Adam was Pure *and* Sinless before God gave him a Helpmate.

And He will be Likewise Again whenever God ceases letting him have a Helpmate any more.

HOLY CITY. CALIFORNIA

Over 500 Different Kinds *of* Post-Cards. All Startling. Priceless Understanding.

Postcard shows Riker had weird views on gender as well as race.

The print shop is seen just beyond the dining room.

Holy City, California

Another small pamphlet published at Holy City was entitled "A Short History of Holy City (no date) - "...Using teams of horses with early-type earth-moving equipment, along with the first steam shovels to be used in the area, the group excavated building sites and erected the first frame buildings near the stand of redwood trees that flourish even today. These buildings were used as quarters for the men and later converted into a restaurant and grocery store. Utilizing the ingenuity of one of its members, the brotherhood constructed a generator which provided current for the first electric lights in the mountains. The group has always been self-sufficient in as much as they raise their own meat, grew their vegetables and fruit, made their own ice, had their own laundry, barber shop, cobbler shop, blacksmith forge and tailor.

"With the advent of the automobile and an all-weather road from San Jose to Santa Cruz, Holy City erected a service station and garage. Business boomed in these two lines due to the fact that there were few such stops on the road...Holy City - 1250 feet above sea level, Average rainfall 40 inches, Average temperature 61 degrees, eleven air miles from the Pacific - On the eastern slopes of the Santa Cruz Mts. Southwestern limits of Santa Clara County. Sun shines on an average of 300 days out of the year. All rainfall is concentrated between the months of October and March, with the greatest amount falling in Dec. and Jan."

At one time there were 14 gas pumps in Holy City to take care of the heavy traffic and tourists.

In November of 1931, the late Howard Sheerin of the *Register-Pajaronian,* attended a meeting of the "Fill-the-Hole Club", an organization of news writers of the Monterey Bay area, at Holy City. "Father" Riker and "Mother" Lucille were the hosts of this gathering and the affair was broadcast over the Holy City radio station, KFQU. "Father Riker and his charming wife went out of their way to give the newspaper folk a time long to be remembered and they succeeded splendidly, it was agreed. The auditorium was tastefully dressed and over the long banquet tables were strung the words 'Welcome, Fill-the-Hole Club'. Fred McPherson, managing editor of the Santa Cruz Sentinel was the toastmaster and the main speaker was Bill Gould of the Pacific Grove newspaper who said: 'I suggest you found a new Holy City along lines which would make it a paradise for newspaper writers. In this new Holy City there would be an ample supply of shirts with sleeves already rolled, and a large supply of eye shades. There

would be no 'deadline' there so that if you didn't feel like working especially hard, we could just take our time and get in our stories whenever we chose...we'd want a murder a day, too. Have them committed just in front of the office so that all we'd have to do would be to sit in the window with our feet propped up and note the details as they occurred.'" - *Evening Pajaronian*, November 23, 1931

John V. Young talks about the same event in *Hot Type & Pony Wire* (1980) - "...Signs of trouble ahead appeared when the first arrivals tasted the punch, served by Mother Riker from two huge cut-glass bowls on an elaborately decorated side table. The punch had all the authority of a W.C.T.U. afternoon tea. A hasty conference in a corner took place, and dollar bills were thrust upon two delegates who disappeared up the highway toward a well-known bootlegger's establishment situated conveniently near by. They soon returned, heavily laden. While the rest of the group diverted the attention of the Rikers on the other side of the room, the delegates spiked the punch. They all but nailed it to the table, for the 'spiking' consisted of two gallons of white mule - colorless, almost tasteless corn whiskey of lethal strength. Mountain people were said to use it as emergency motor fuel and reported phenomenal performance from their vehicles as a result.

"Suitably diluted in the punch, it went down without a whisper, and as stealthily sneaked up on the unwary consumers; namely the Rikers. The club members worked in relays, offering toasts to everyone they could think of, and of course to be good hosts the Rikers had to chug-a-lug at each toast. It was not long before Mother Riker excused herself and disappeared, and a little later Father Riker floated away to his couch...."

The name "Fill-the-Hole-Club" comes from when advertisements are inserted into a newspaper, the leftover space is called the "hole" and a reporter's job is to "fill-the-hole".

"'Papa' Riker in Car Upset, Los Gatos, April 21, William Edgar (sic) Riker, 'father' of Holy City near here, overturned his car in a near accident on the south edge of the city today. Riker admitted to Chief of Police Henry C. Noble that he was driving on the wrong side at a curve of the highway when a car containing four women coming from the south appeared. To avoid hitting them, he swerved to his own side of the road, and in doing so turned his car over on the side. The damage was inconsiderable. Riker was unhurt." - *San Jose Mercury Herald*, April 22, 1934

The following is from the *San Francisco Chronicle*, August 14, 1934 - "Isaiah's Flock To Get Home - Holy City August 13th - Members of the Holy City flock of 'Father' Riker will leave this week to confer with members of the cult of the late Brother Isaiah at Oroville seeking to get them to join the Holy City colony. 'I will have them here if they will shave off their beards and cut their hair.' Riker says. Members of brother Isaiah's colony thought him immortal. He preached to them that he was, but when he died recently he failed to revive and authorities forced his followers to bury him." Riker toured Isaiah Cudney's colony of "Immortals" but evidently Isaiah's flock didn't like Riker's "suggestions" as nothing came of the idea.

Later that year, on December 24th, the following appeared in the *San Francisco Chronicle:* "Holy City Chief Hurt in Crash - Father W.E. Riker, picturesque head of the Holy City colony in the Santa Cruz mountains, received a broken leg and other hurts when his auto collided with that of Robert D. Durham of San Francisco on the highway near Mt. View. Durham received internal injuries and his wife a broken leg. Donald Dencole, 35, and Albert Thiele, Holy City colonists, received head injuries; all are at Mt. View Hospital."

"Fred Rommel, driver for the Holy City Bottling Works, Wednesday morning paid a fine of $100 when, accompanied to court by 'Holy Joe' (Joe Albert), assistant of W.E. Riker, he pleaded quilty to driving while under the influence of liquor.   Rommel, after 10:30 p.m. Tuesday, drove a truck load of empty bottles against a highway sign at the foot of El Monte hill. No one was hurt." - *Los Gatos Times*, October 23, 1936

In 1937, Riker stated to Muriel Rukeyser of the Los Angeles *Times:* Yes, I used to be a show man, spent several years at that and several more wandering around the middle west and then for awhile I was a teacher. You might call me a teacher now. But I can't say I'm a bookish man, though. Haven't read more than three books in my whole life. If I believed I could find what I'm looking for in books I'd go straight to them, but books can't do that for me." In 1938 there were 75 men and 4 women living at Holy City.

A sign displayed at Holy City, probably in 1938 when Riker first ran for Governor of California, proclaimed:

Positively, neither candidate will ever make good unless in them accepting the herein mentioned true solutions to those certain great problems that positively have to become correctly solved before any peace and success can ever be in this world. The cat is now out of the bag! (drawing of a cat coming out of a bag).

No.1 No longer are those murderous wars needed because we now have the true solution to get rid of them.

No.2 No longer are our imperfect governments needed because we now have the perfected one to take their places.

No.3 No longer do our intelligent people have to tolerate terrible-God race crime blood mixing because we have the true solution to that racial problem.

No.4 Also we now have the true solution to that spiritual religious problem as never before in history.

No.5 If in any doubt, please investigate and be sure and read the book. It is a real miracle book.

Be sure to attend free public meetings each Sunday 8 p.m. at Holy City.

THE EMANCIPATOR

25c

Cover of the Holy City publication, The Emancipator.

He published a twenty-page pamphlet entitled *The Emancipator* which sold for 25 cents. This publication was published in 1938 and talks of his being a candidate for Governor of California. He ran unsucessfully for this office four times - 1938, 1942, 1946 and 1950. Following are some quotes from *The Emancipator* as espoused by the very bigoted William Riker: "The White Man can take care of any and all kinds of business in our own, White Man's California State Home, and no longer will the White Man tolerate your undermining and polluting tactics. Farmers, Business Men and the Workers say: Orientals get out and stay out of our business. Our new Government will see that you get a job. Your polluting, undermining system of business must eternally stop in Our California And besides this, keep your polluting hands off our White Race Women; they also belong only to the White Race Man. This is the true law of our Original White Man's CONSTITUTION, these statements explain the real and true spirit of California."

"California has a disgraceful, criminal, cesspool system of Government. With a man at the head of it who is not a native of California and without any true solution for this cesspool condition and what is more, it is getting worse every minute and for sure will cause the State to crack up, unless the people of California harken to William E. Riker who has the true solutions for all of our problems and can make the State of California Paradise to live in."

Some of these pamphlets were illustrated by Basil G. Wolverton who later became an illustrator for *Mad* magazine. Another artist was Professor S. Brickman, whose address was listed as Holy City and whose strange pictures appear in *The Emancipator.*

HEADQUARTERS
THE NEW WORLD CHRISTIAN RELIGION
INCORPORATED

SUN. EVE. 8 P.M.   ADM. FREE

DO NOT KID YOURSELF....
THAT ANY PRESENT DAY GOVERNMENT
OR RELIGION WILL EVER BRING ANY
PEACE IN THIS WORLD BECAUSE BOTH
ARE GROSSLY IGNORANT IN THAT WAY.
BLAME ONLY THEM & NOT THE DEVIL
FOR ALL THE HELL ON EARTH !

Some of the signs at Holy City, found later in the Riker house attic.

CHAPTER V

THE WORLD WAR II YEARS

Started in the 1930s, Highway 17 opened officially from Santa Cruz to Los Gatos in 1940; America entered World War II in 1941 and on December 1, 1942, gas rationing went into effect and Holy City began its' downward slide. But not without a lot of effort on Riker's part to divert traffic to his "kingdom." He was constantly putting up more signs and spouting his philosophy around the Santa Clara valley. But this was war time and people were short on gas and worried about the future. When and if they heard or saw 'Father' Riker, they looked upon him as that "crazy" man.

All the men that worked at Holy City were not disciples. A case in point was Andy Desin of Los Gatos who, in 1940 worked in the Holy City bar and coffee shop and lived upstairs in the hotel. He tells of Riker coming into the bar one day and spotting a bottle of Black & White labeled scotch. He said that would never do and told Desin to turn the bottle around so the label would not show - showing his extreme prejudice. Desin also played softball with the Hillbillies who were sponsored by the Sunshine Club of Holy City. Their games were

The "Drinks 5¢ and 10¢ Barbecue" stayed the same, but the two pictures show the change from religion to politics, as "Heaven" and the angels are painted over in favor of Riker and "U.S. Government/ Banking Business." Notice the Santas, far left.

held at the Los Gatos high school field. When he was at Holy City, Dave Arnwine leased the gas station and Morris Lawrence leased the bar and restaurant.

From the *San Jose Mercury Herald*, October 14, 1942: "As it did in the garden of Eden, the red hand of murder struck yesterday in picturesque Holy City in the hills above Los Gatos, leaving one man dead, another critically injured and sending squads of Sheriff William J. Emig's deputies scouring the rugged mountain country of the region in search of the accused killer.

"Fatally bludgeoned with an iron bar during an argument over how emergency fire ladders were to be constructed on Holy City buildings was Joseph Witzig, 58, a carpenter. He died in the Santa Clara County hospital shortly after being clubed by I.B. Fisher, 60, another carpenter who also seriously injured Arthur Kastner, 62, a third workman, before running away into the mountains, Sheriff Emig reported."

Riker was worried about enemy planes coming over Holy City; dropping bombs and starting fires on roofs so he had instructed Witzig and Kastner to place ladders on the sides of buildings for easy access in case of fire. When they approached Fisher he flew into a rage with the above results. He eventually returned to Holy City and turned himself in and was sentenced to five years at San Quentin. After serving two and a half years, he was parolled and warned to stay away from Holy City. He moved into a small house on Summit Road and died in 1980 at the age of 98.

In 1942, the Federal Bureau of Investigation brought 'Father' Riker to trial for sedition. He had been writing letters to Hitler and publishing very questionable pamphlets. "Holy City 'King' jailed by FBI - 'Father' William E. Riker, perennial candidate for governor and 'King' of the Holy City colony in the Santa Cruz mountains, was arrested late Thursday by the FBI on a sedition indictment. He was charged with calling Adolph Hitler 'a second Martin Luther,' urging congressmen to make peace with the Axis and distributing propaganda labeled as anti-semitic, anti-British, anti-Chinese and anti-Filipino." *Register Pajaronian*, October 31, 1942. He fired his first attorney and hired Melvin Belli of San Francisco for the sum of $7,500; $2,500 to be paid up front and the balance of $5,000 at the end of the trial.

Riker with attorney Melvin Belli.

Riker Free, But Gives Up Pamphlets

SAN FRANCISCO (UP) Wil liam E. Riker, who claims to be the "wise man of the west" but is "the screwiest of screwballs in his attorney's opinion, stood exoner ated Saturday of sedition charges

Even so, the 68-year-old patri arch of Holy City will write no more pamphlets for the duration, he said, after a jury of six men and six women acquitted him in federal court late Friday night

"I never committed any crime, but I'm not going to write any more pamphlets for the dura tion," he said, mopping his brow and nodding at the members of the jury.

"To the world I say, 'I want the Jews and gentiles to get together spiritually to live a human bible '"

Although the government is through with Riker, the sect lead er has an issue to settle with Fa ther Divine, the Philadelphia ne gro cultist.

He said he and his attorney, Melvin Belli, would go to New York immediately and file a suit for criminal libel against the Peace-It's-Wonderful leader He blamed Father Divine for his trou ble with the Federal Bureau of In vestigation.

Register Pajaronian has some fun reporting Riker's acquittal.

Riker was acquitted and chastised; he left the
courtroom with a small American flag in his pocket and
climbed into his red, white and blue sedan saying:
"...there will be no question of his unmitigated
patriotism or love of country." When Belli tried to
collect the $5,000 balance of his fee he was told: "My son,
I shall reward you with a seat in my kingdom in
Heaven and that is far more emolument than a paltry
$5,000, mere money." Belli had to sue for the money and
won in May of 1943.

"Storm clouds are brewing in the Holy City paradise
of 'Father' William E. Riker and over the New York
heavens of 'Father' Divine, the diminutive dusky 'god'
of thousands of harlems 'angels.' In an affidavit filed
with the Federal Court here yesterday, Melvin Belli,
attorney for Riker, charged Divine with inspiring the
arrest and indictment of Riker on charges of sedition.
The motive, according to Belli, jealousy - 'Father Divine
is jealous because Father Riker has used the name
Father and calls himself 'The Wise Man of the West',
whereas Father Divine claims he is the one wise man,
and, in fact, claims he is God....'" - *San Francisco
Chronicle* December 6, 1942

" William E. Riker of Holy City, perennial candidate
for Governor, yesterday qualified with Secretary of State
Jordan on both the Republican and Democratic tickets at
June 4th elections. His platform, as indicated in his paid
ads, stresses the racial issues. He wants to protect the
white race from all others." - *San Francisco Chronicle,*
March 22, 1946
He lost.

CHAPTER VI

POST-WAR DECLINE

In December of 1947, Riker's son, Bill, was savagely beaten as he left a bar in San Jose. Found at his small house by officer Neece, who had followed a trail of blood, Riker had a broken ankle, head and chest wounds, plus other injuries sustained from being beaten and kicked. Young Riker was working as a hod carrier and had left Holy City some years before. He claimed that three men had jumped him trying to force him back to the "fold". Though he claimed that one of the men was a cult member, he refused to identify him saying "he would have killed me if I did." Several days after the incident, a laborer was jailed by the name of Jack Cobrunson, 25, whom Riker identified as one of his assailants. Not much is known about Francois (Bill) except that he served in World War II and his address was listed as the U.S. Navy Recruiting Office in Seattle. In 1957 he went to court claiming that his father was not fit to run his estate but Judge W.W. Jacks ruled that 'Father' Riker was not incompetent.

From "Freddie Francisco Observes", *San Francisco Chronicle,* April 22, 1948 - "... The only establishment in town which still looks prosperous and well-kept is the

Comforter's home which stands on a knoll at the head
of the main and only street. Riker took care of Riker. A
mere twenty of the original 200 converts remain in the
colony and most of these totter, vacant eyed and cane
supported through the deserted village. One of these
the Comforter found waiting for him outside his house
one morning not so long ago. He was hanging, dead,
from a tree which stands at his doorway."

Riker's home in later years.

On July 4th, 1950, 'Mother' Lucille suffered a stroke
and was in a coma until she died on July 13th at the
Spottswood Rest Home in Los Gatos. She was buried at
the IOOF Cemetery in Santa Cruz. Lucille Jensen was
born January 1, 1874 in Lincoln, Nebraska and became
Riker's helpmate from the time of their marriage in 1914
until her death. She appeared to always be dedicated to
his cause and stood by him through thick and thin.

John McNicholas of the Santa Cruz *Sentinel*
interviewed Connie Kidwell of Campbell (who used to
live off Greenwood Drive near Holy City) in March of
1991, on the subject of Holy City: "There was a lot of
skulduggery that went on up there. I went to a couple of
Father Riker's meetings and was at his very last meeting
at Holy City. He was a fat man, and he'd sit up there and
burp, with a little beanie on his head...He was a
lecherous old guy. All the ladies had to sleep with
Father Riker first...I didn't think he was a good looking
man; he might have been when he was young, but he
was nothing much to look at."

In 1956 Maurice Kline, a musical director from
Hollywood, became Riker's partner and was proclaimed
the new "Jewish Messiah" of Holy City by Riker. He also
became the owner of half of Holy City due to 'Father's'
largess (which he later regretted.) On the night of June
17, 1957, a large hall at Holy City was reduced to rubble by
fire. Earl Russell, custodian and Emil Reichsteiner,
barber, who made their home in the building, escaped
unharmed. Kline said that much of Riker's writings
were consumed in the flames (not a tremendous loss!).
The cult leader was then in a rest home recovering from
a broken hip, the result of another auto accident.

Robert Clogher, public relations director of the
National Nudist Council and former personal secretary
to Riker, was the self-appointed, acting Safety Patrol
Chief at Holy City. He wanted to make the area a nudist
colony but that idea was never carried through. In fact,
Riker tossed Clogher out in August of 1958 along with
Jim Wood, a former disciple.

Later that same year Kline purchased the other half

of the acreage that made up the Holy City area for $64,000. Riker agreed to the terms of the sale whereby they would not "be allowed to preach any philosophy although they may remain as residents of the area if they desire." By December Riker was regretting the sale and went to the Santa Clara superior Court for the return of the property. In February of 1959 the State of California handed down the decision that Kline was indeed the owner of Holy City.

From the *Los Gatos-Saratoga Times Observor,* August 7, 1957 - "Harmony in Holy City Again - Harmony returned to Holy City last week when Joseph Albert, a disciple of the community brotherhood, withdrew his suit against William E. 'Father' Riker and Maurice Kline. This unison was demonstrated at a luncheon meeting with Kline and six disciples who selected Miss Winifred Allington, retired Holy City postmaster, as their spokesman. After hearing Kline, new owner of Holy City, outline and express his hopes for the future, Mrs. Allington declared: 'We all are very well satisfied with the change and feel that at last we are on the main track. We have been on detour long enough....'

"The attorney (Stoner) further stated that the seven other remaining disciples also each accepted a promissory note for $8,000 as his share of the $64,000 sale. Each may elect to receive payment as he desires, he said. The others, in addition to Riker, are Rozum and Miss Allington, Emil Reichsteiner, barber; Fred Rommel, electrician; Arthur Landstrum, clerk; and David L. Capps, maintenance employee. All were present at the luncheon except Landstrum and Riker, the latter still in hospital after injuries suffered in an automobile accident in May. Albert will manage the Holy City Tavern, now being remodeled and redecorated according to Kline."

From the *San Francisco Chronicle*, "This World", August 10, 1958: "One of the few cheerful persons around the place (Holy City) is Winifred Allington, who at 78 is the last of the women Disciples. 'Miss Ally', as she is known, lives with her 30 cats and complete peace of mind. But what of working all her life with nothing at the end to show for it? 'I was postmistress here for many years and I have a little pension,' she said. 'It's enough to feed me and my cats and that's all I need. What I've given here was in the nature of a contribution and I never expected anything back on it. Of course,' she added with a smile, 'if they are going to cut up the pie, I'd like a piece.' Whom was she suing, if anyone? 'Well, to tell you the truth, I'm really not sure at the moment.' she said with a chuckle that came from deep within her. 'There's so many suits around that you can't tell the players without a program.'"

Kline was to raze a number of buildings in 1959 including the observatory and radio station. The restaurant was still functioning and became known as "Poor Richards." In August another fire leveled a two-story building built in the early 20s and which had been topped by a cupola; it had housed the printing office, barber shop and ice plant.

"Firebug on Loose In Holy City - A firebug apparently is on the loose in Holy City. Jim Edmondson, who runs the garage at Holy City, reported that he received an anonymous call Thursday from a caller who threatened to set fire to the garage. A Wednesday fire had already caused about $2,500 damage to the garage and another building. It was the second major fire in three months at Holy City. Tuesday Maurice Kline, who has title to the settlement, reported that he received threats by mail and telephone that the community would be burned. These threats were not anonymous, said Kline, and he turned over the caller's name to authorities. Kline said flatly that both Wednesday's fire and the one in August were arson. An arson investigation is being held." *Register Pajaronian* October 30, 1959

The August 31, 1959 fire that burned two-thirds of the buildings.

A man was brought in and questioned but no proof of his being involved in the fires was proved so he was released. In 1960 the property, now 140 acres, was purchased by the H.C. Development Company of San Jose who had plans to develop the area but it was well on its way to becoming a ghost town; at least in comparison to what it once was.

The following appeared in the *Register Pajaronian* on July 29, 1966 - "Holy City Founder Converted - 'Father' William E. Riker, founder of Holy City, a cultist retreat off Highway 17 south of Los Gatos, yesterday was conditionally baptized as a Catholic. Riker, who is 94, and used to call himself 'The wisest man on earth' and the leader of 'the way' said of his becoming a Catholic 'I was intelligently converted. I've been living a celibate life for ten years." At the time of his conversion Riker was confined to a wheelchair as the result of a stroke. Witnessing the ceremony were two of his first disciples, Irwin Fisher, 85 and Stephen Rozum, 81.

One of the few signs found later by Mary Starke in the attic of Riker's former house in Holy City: "Noah Announced the Flood and the Messiah is now announncing the plague to sweep the earth. Noah got the animals together and the Messiah will get the surviving mankind together in their proper place after the plague." But mankind was no longer listening. Riker had become a doddering old man; his wife, "Mother" Lucille was gone; most of the disciples had moved away or were dead. His holy kingdom had crumbled and the world had passed him by leaving him with a mixture of fading memories.

"Father" William Riker

CHAPTER VII

ENDINGS

William Riker died on December 3, 1969, 7:08 a.m. at Agnews State Hospital, Ward 87, at 96 years of age. Immediate cause of death, Cardiac arrest. According to the *San Francisco Examiner*, "he was sent (to Agnews) four months ago because of his extreme age and inability to get along with anyone in private rest homes." The information on his death certificate was provided by his nephew, Ray Riker of San Jose. The whereabouts of Riker's son was unknown at the time. At the time of Riker's death, there were reputed to be three disciples left in Holy City.

From the *Register Pajaronian* December 5, 1969: "It must have been about 15 years ago. A long black sedan slid into two parking spaces just outside the window of what then was my office. It was an ancient thing, but I recognized it immediately - because I, too, had once driven a LaSalle. The LaSalle disgorged an old man of obvious dignity, who wanted to see me on some pressing problem or other, the nature of which escapes me now. I think it was something about the state government or some other collection of miscreants. We had a pleasant visit, and I marveled at the sharpness of the old man's mind, his command of the English language.

Riker's uniqueness: Who else combined "General Merchandise," "Free Auto Camp," and "Public Comfort Station" with "Heaven" and "Future Generations is not the wise man's way?"

"That was William Edward Riker, 'Father' Riker. He died this week in Ward 87 of Agnews State Hospital at the age of 96. Even in death the old eccentric left a problem. He had been converted to Roman Catholicism three years ago. His wife and some of his early disciples are buried in the Odd Fellows Cemetery in Santa Cruz, but there's no plot for the old man, his newphew reported. Sad." - Frank Orr, former editor

But he was buried there along with 'Mother' Lucille and three women disciples: Emma Phillips D: 1956; Anna Schramm D: 1953 and Emma Stauff D: 1955. In 1970 Joe Albert and Harry Reynolds were living in Riker's home atop the knoll in Holy City. From September 1979 to September of 1980, Mary Starke of Campbell rented the Riker house and tells of how run-down it was and badly in need of repair. The old house still has a tenant with several large dogs guarding the premises.

Holy city was often referred to as a religious cult but that was certainly a misnomer. Riker's "teachings" were more philosophy than anything else. His was a very strange and queer way of thinking on many, many subjects. He was against families living together at Holy City but lived with his wife in a comfortable house atop a knoll overlooking his "kingdom". The "disciples" he had gathered around him were mostly all men; they received no pay, just room and board and did all the menial jobs around the property. And what was Riker doing? Taking in over $100,000 a year in the organization's heyday; spewing out his biased and off-beat philosophy to anyone who would listen. He handed out his inflamatory pamphlets and tracts while walking around Holy City, to the thousands of tourists who poured through the village. They were there because the main road betwen Santa Cruz and San Jose ran through Holy City but they stopped mostly out of curiosity. The place exuded a carnival atmosphere and motorists wanted to see what it was all about. They often went away shaking their heads in disbelief as they headed on to a seemingly saner world.

Riker was a charlaton, a bigot and most certainly, and undeniably, unique. His ideas were a mixture of radical thinking and a narrow mind; the older he became, the worse it got. He was full of ideas and suggestions for everyone and about everything from how to treat women to how to run the government. He was an insatiable writer of letters, preaching his point of view on any subject imaginable. Most of his writings were way out in left field - no one there to catch the ball or even wanting to!

The more one delves into the man's personna, the more crazy and confused he seems. Why these "disciples", mostly men, were attracted to his philosophy is very hard to understand and yet, understandable in a way. These people were usually down on their luck, roaming men who needed someone to follow as had happened in so many other cases. Holy City was at its height just before and during the depression and prohibition. These factors plus a circus type atmosphere and being located on the main road led to the "success" of Holy City. Now virtually a ghost town, except for Stanton's Holy City Art Glass Company, it still brings back memories to many people of an earlier day, when the "King", the "Comforter" of the "Perfect Government" and the "Perfect Christian Divine Way" strolled through his "Holy" kingdom contemplating his next lecture or pamphlet that would espouse his divine teachings and bring more monies into his own pockets. But the money seemed to spill out just as quickly as it came in.

Holy City Art Glass (building on right) is the only business that remains in the "ghost town" today.

Overgrown approach to Holy City, 1992.

"Holy City is the Comforter and the new Jerusalem. The city is a place where we claim we solve all problems. It's a philosophy based on wisdom, not education. There's nothing to study. You just lay quiet and learn what you already know in you. Some religions claim you go to heaven when you croak. Well, that's a fish story."

"Father" William Riker

The Riker home today, kept hidden by the overgrowth.

APPENDIX I

CONCERNING PENSIONS
(article from the *Los Gatos Times*, November 25, 1938)

Father Riker, Holy City man, has caused to be sent to us an 8-page paper which explains his attitude toward various social and economic problems of the day. Father Riker has conceived of a perfect pension plan, he says, and in line with his old established policy he is offering a reward to those who can find a flaw in it. Evidently the problem of conceiving a pension plan has been a vexing one to Father Riker, for while he is putting up one thousand bucks for the flat-foot floogie who can find a flaw, his $25,000 reward to those who can say, truthfully, that his perfect form of government is even tinctured with boloney, is still standing. The difference between $1000 and $25,000 is considerable, and to us, at least, is an indication that possibly Father Riker has his private doubts about his pension plan. We cannot see any reason why the Holy City seer should not be willing to post $25,000 for those who can riddle his pension plan. That he failed to do so is an indication to us that his latest plan is not as good as the previously expounded perfect-form-of-government plan. Of course, those who go out to seek these rewards should bear in mind that the only way that Father Riker's theories can be disproved is by large scale, practical application. The catch, as we see it, is that Father Riker's perfect government plan would have to be put in effect in a big way.

Father Riker, along with two other fellows named Merriam and Olson, was a candidate for governor in the last election. His defeat by Mr. Olson is accounted for in Point 7 of Father Riker's paper, under the general heading of "William E. Riker Has Come To Cure the Curse of California." Point 7 states: "he (Father Riker) was not the citizen's choice since ninety per cent of the citizen's did not give William E. Riker and some others a chance to explain themselves, their message and platform. The fact is evident, our present system of stealing into the office is un-American and un-Democratic. It must stop."

Father Riker's pension plan is outlined in four fabulous phases on page two of his paper. Here they are:

Here is a true solution for all disabled and pension-minded people, and is one that none can legitimately complain about, or will it ever meet with successful opposition. Positively it is the only true plan that will agreeably work.

1st. Phase: First of all it takes care of all needy and disabled people regardless of age. Second, it would be imposssible for anyone receiving a pension to abuse its sacred cause. Third, it will be impossible for any graft or racketeering to develop among those who administer this particular service. After understanding this plan, for sure it will satisfy the minds of all people.

2nd. Phase: The amount of money needed for pensions including the expense of its administration will be raised by issuing State pension stamps and these stamps will be purchased by every merchant and business institution within the boundaries of the State. These stamps will be supplied through local banks and have to be pasted and cancelled on every business transaction and the amount of the cancelled pasted stamps will be collected by purchasers. Should stamps be sold out befoe the end of the year, no more stamps need to be purchased until the following year. Surplus stamps will be exchanged for new ones. The price of the stamps will be determined later.

3rd. Phase: Social doctors will be employed to prescribe the just and proper treatment and medicine for his patient. According to anyone's social, physical and mental circumstances, the social doctors will determine the necessary amount to be prescribed. These social doctors are paid to treat each patient with the greatest of consideration, so that the social doctor as well as the State will be honored as good social fatherly physicians. Those receiving pensions, who are qualified, will be employed to act as administrators.

4th. Phase: Owing to the many abuses and poor judgment that might develop with some who receive pensions, they will be given a checkbook to write out checks for what is purchased. This system will be a tell-tale of those who are guilty of abusing the sacred cause of receiving pensions. Also a full check will be kept and openly published regarding every detail of its entire administration. Any abuse or violation on the part of anyone will cause their pension to be differently adjusted.

APPENDIX II

LETTER TO SOVIET PREMIER
(from a pamphlet, mid-1950's)

His Excellency,
Premier G. M. Malenkov,
The Kremlin, Moscow
Union of Soviet Socialist Republics.
Your Excellency:

Decided to write you an interesting letter, besides sending you a couple of copies of special letters that I wrote and sent to our President of the United States; and also copy of a letter sent to the Chief Justice in the U.S. Supreme Court, in belief that you will enjoy reading them. These same kind of copies have also been sent to many other big officials that sit in the saddle throughout the world.

I somewhat explain myself in this letter to you. I surely would like to meet and talk to you as I have all of the many all-new arguments to interest you with. I claim that the whole world is going up Smoke Creek if those big boys don't find out the True Solution in the near future and as you know, in mechanical ways and in science, some people are quite smart; but in social and political construction they are more blind than are some animals.

I fully realize that you belong to the white-race of people as I do; and all of us white-race people must cease being enemies to one another and come under One Flag in all co-operative brotherly oneness. This can easily be done when it is decided upon with proper understanding and intelligent leadership.

After reading my two copies of letters, if you are able to drop me a few lines and ask me to go see someone, I will do so, and perhaps we may become profitably acquainted. I will be glad to answer all questions and to play my part for the sake of Eternal Peace on this Earth.

Here are four points to wisely consider in becoming progressive, beautiful in thought and spirit, according to the principals of Holy City:

No. 1 Any government that is not yet perfect, must naturally act like an immature man. It is wise to let it carry on until mature while at the same time it must continue to try to improve itself if possible until it develops in the fullness of mature perfection. It is also wisdom to let the people who support it, decide through democratic processes, to either carry on with it or to change over to a different plan and form of successful working government, particularly so, to the one that does the most for its people.

No. 2 As is a foot-race conducted with different entries, in fact that same principle should likewise be carried out with all different governments in trying to win first place in doing the most for its people, while following a certain decided time that is allowed for one and all to demonstrate themselves, and the one that achieves the most for its people is the only thing that gives good reasons for all the others to follow up in that same pattern, whether it be the final and perfect plan or not.

No. 3 Overlook not in this latter-day that soon it will be known which people and which country is the most progressive, honest, considerate, open-minded and also willing to do what is right at any cost, and such a government and its people will likewise become Divinely credited as the champion winner in that good and particular respect. Let each individual government and its people strive to be successful in that way, so in the end through such striving and success, there will consequently be but One Perfect Plan of Government and Religion for all its civilized people to both glorify this wonderful world and also all mankind, as was intended from the very beginning.

No. 4 Finally the fourth and great thing to achieve, is to bring or to cause all of the different nationalities of the Great Gentile white-race of people throughout this world, to be and to come under one all-new White-Race Man beautiful flag, and also in practice a 100 percent brotherhood, co-operation and dependable partnership in this all great and final business of trying to please both God and also all mankind, that is sure to cause a 100 per cent honey-making situation and condition to come and be in this entire world, that is also symbolic to a honey-making beehive with its all-inspiring and life-giving Queen Bee that rules in her honey-making hive. The only side-kick partner of the entirity of the Queen Bee Great Gentile white race people and all the others as a whole, are the Great Jewish People, as does the head on your shoulders, that acts as an intermediator between the center, the trunk of the physical body and the limbs. In other words the Jewish and Gentile White Race People will spiritually unite and become not only the Human Bible for all mankind, but also the Royal Family of God in both ruling all mankind and also in raising them up into equal position.

If interested please contact this particular author and man to give you both free and also full information. Also remember, when this is and will be achieved, it is only then it will all greater and lesser in position races of people become fully pleased, and they will also experience Eternal Peace for all time to come in this world, which is the Divine Duty for all great men and leaders to work for and to achieve in this world, when in winding them up, their conscience wiil be 100 percent clear.

Respectfully submitted,
Father W.E. Riker
Founder of Holy City,
California
U.S.A.

APPENDIX III

THE EMANCIPATOR
(two items from the pamphlet, 1939)

The Truth and Nothing but the Truth

Chasing the Devil Around the Stump, Explains Our United States Democracy.

Going From Bad to Worse.

This Picture explains our U. S. Democratic Government in action.

Explains
Dictatorship

The Devil Captured But Not Conquered.

This Picture explains the Government of Germany.

William E. Riker Conquers the Devil

THROUGH THE PERFECT GOVERNMENT

This Picture explains William E. Riker's Perfect System of Government.

$25,000 REWARD

If you can find a flaw in William E. Riker's Perfect System of Government and prove it will not work.

He says it is fundamentally criminally wrong to allow either private banking or insurance, or allow the neglect of disabled citizens, unemployment, and undermining polluting race crime.

Through his Perfect form of Government crime, wars, strikes and depressions will be abolished. His system does everything without any trouble. Be sure and read all of his literature, where everything is explained in simple language. in nugget form.

William E. Riker is the only man who has a true solution and knows how to be a real California Governor for our glorious State of California.

Here are six outstanding ideas that will surely go down in history:

No. 1. The problems of your home and family are no different than in your home city, state and its citizens.

No. 2. Your own home that you cherish and live in, and your home City and State, are no different. They are one institution.

No. 3. What will crack up a home will also crack up your home city and state.

No. 4. What a good father will not stand for in his home, neither would a good Governor stand for our California state home. *Real Californians must run California and not across the line foreigners.*

No. 5. William E. Riker guarantees to convert any one, in five minutes to his plan and solution.

No. 6. If you don't want me to be the Governor, I want You to be, if you will carry out this plan. Our slogan, to all California citizens is, Hello! Governor.

BIBLIOGRAPHY

"California's Holy City," 8/22/1937, *Los Angeles Times* by Muriel Rukeyser

American Weekly, Inc., 1938, "'King' Riker's 'Holy City'"

Sacramento Bee, Feb. 24, 1950, "Office Seeker Urges Racial Segregations"

Fortnight, 3/2/1955, "Holy City Brotherhood" by Bill Sumner pgs 16 & 17

S.C. Sentinel, 6/18/1957, Holy City fire

S.C. Sentinel, 7/25/1957, Maurice Kline purchases half of Holy City

Santa Cruz Sentinel, 8/31/1959, "Fire Razes Building in Holy City"

Sacramento Bee, 5/13/1960, "Developer Buys Holy City Site in Santa Clara"

San Francisco Examiner, 1961, "Carnival and Cultism in the Santa Cruz Mountains - The Holy City" by Walter Blum

San Francisco Examiner, 12/4/1969, pg. 55, Riker obituary

San Jose Mercury, 12/5/1969, pg. 36, Riker obituary

Ventura County Star, "Once Colorful Holy City Fades into Ghost Town", by Wally Smith, 4/5/1970

California Today, 8/30/1970, "Riker: From Mechanic to Messiah" by Harry Plate

Signs Of the Times, "The Sad Story Of the City Men Built," May 1972

New World Utopias, by Paul Kagan, Penguin 1975 pgs 102 - 117

San Jose News, 1/16/1976, "Holy City Joins Ghostly Ranks" by Patricia Loomis

My Life On Trial, by Melvin Belli, 1976 Wm. Morrow & Co.

Trailblazer, 11/1978, "Wm. E. Riker's Holy City," pg. 3

Monterey Peninsula Herald - Weekender, 10/14/1979, "Holy City - Father Riker's Unholy Experiment," James Denison

KOMY Radio Station, Watsonville, "'Father' William Riker" 2/11/1980 by Betty Lewis

Los Gatos Times Observor, "Once a Thriving Town, Holy City Long Forgotten," by Evelyn Gallagher, 1/4/1980

Hot Type & Pony Wire, by John V. Young, 1980, pgs 31-42

California, Inc., 1982, Joel Kotkin & Paul Grabowicz, pg 156

California's Utopian Colonies, by Robert V. Hine, 1983, U.C. Press, Berkeley

Los Gatos Weekly, "The Strange Saga of Holy City," Jon Carroll, 3/2/83

West, "Salvation Circus," Nov. 1984, by Barbara Bailey Kelley

Ghost Towns of the Santa Cruz Mountains, 1984, by John V. Young
     pgs 31-34

"The Holy City Sideshow," 4/20/1988 by Joan Barriga

"Holy City" May 1988 by Betty Lewis, San Jose Historical Museum
     Publication

San Jose: A Personal View, 1989 by Wes Payton

Santa Cruz Sentinel, "Holy City," by Betty Lewis, March 31, 1991

RIKER'S PUBLICATIONS

The Emancipator, pamphlet published by Riker, no date

Copies of three very important letters by Wm. Riker (no date)

The Final Wisdom & Understanding For You, no date, $1.00, published
     by the Holy City Press at Holy City, Alma, P.O. CA (booklet);

> "Mortal woman is man's only legitimate enemy, and mortal
> man is her only legitimate undeveloped child. In the end, when
> developed, both will be human beings at peace, and not arguing
> men and women."

*Holy City in God's Country CALIFORNIA; The Spiritual Melting Pot
     of U.S.,* 8 pages, no date;

> "If you haven't a mind and spirit like a German do not expect
> to know what he is saying, likewise if you haven't a mind and
> spirit like Jesus Christ do not expect to know what he is talking
> about."

> "According to Holy City, womankind is the GOD of this
> World. The rejected Jew is the SOUL of this World, the Gentile
> white man is the New Born Child soon to glorify IT. The Black
> and Yellow skin people are the Sacred Servants of these people.
> The Hindu blue skin and the Red man are in retrogression for some
> time yet to come and must be directed by those above."

Map of Holy City, card, no date

The Cause of Infantile Paralysis Explained, booklet, 14 pgs., $1.00,
     no date

"other books available:

1. The Perfect System of Government .25 cents

2. The Great Eye Opener 1.00

3. The Master Mind Discipleship Book 1.00

4. The Great Jewish People .50 cents
5. The Whole Truth & Nothing But the Truth 1.00
6. The Real Cause of Infantile...
    "Send $3.00 for all books"

The Perfect Government, booklet, 16 pages, no date
The Book of Books That Surely Sizzles with the Final Wisdom of God
Diamond Key Book, Ten Commandments For Women
A Short History Of Holy City, no date

CREDITS

Special Thanks To: Carl Balch, Bill Balch, Judge John Ball, Joan
    Barriga, Richard Beal, Virginia Coleman, James Denison, Andrew
    Desin, Willie Frank, Bruce Franks, Will Irvick, Paul Kagan,
    Connie Kidwell, John McNicholas, Leo Pelochotti, William
    Sheehy, Alzora Snyder, Tom Stanton, Mary Starke, Gary Strong,
    Paul VonAhnen, Bob Wilson and John V. Young
Photographs: Carroll Cross, Myrtle Brady, Diane Varni, James
    Denison, Mary Starke, and Jim Thompson, Wide World Photos,
    and *San Francisco Chronicle*.

Sources:
Webster's American Biographies, 1975, Chas. Van Doren, Robert
    McHenry
University of California at Santa Cruz, Special Collections
California State Library, Gary Strong and staff, Sacramento
Watsonville City Library
Alameda County Library
San Jose Historical Museum Association
Bancroft Library, University of California at Berkeley
Los Gatos Times Observor
Evening Pajaronian, Watsonville, California
Santa Cruz Sentinel
San Jose Mercury News
San Francisco Chronicle
San Francisco Examiner

INDEX

Topics in
Monterey Bay Area History

A Series of Works That Explore Specific Themes in &
Around Santa Cruz and Monterey Counties.

Published by OTTER B BOOKS:
Forever Facing South: The Story of the S.S. Palo Alto,
    The Old Cement Ship of Seacliff Beach;
    David W. Heron
Californians: Searching for the Golden State;
    James D. Houston
Holy City: Riker's Roadside Attraction; Betty Lewis

Distributed by OTTER B BOOKS:
Chinese Gold: The Chinese in the Monterey Bay Region;
    Sandy Lydon
Monterey in 1786: The Journals of Jean François
    de La Pérouse
Lighthouse Point: Reflections on Monterey Bay History;
    Frank Perry
A Howling Wilderness: Summit Road to 1906;
    Stephen Payne
A Wild Coast and Lonely: Big Sur Pioneers; R.S. Wall
Monterey Bay Area: Natural History and Cultural
    Imprints; Burton L. Gordon
Santa Cruz County Place Names; Donald T. Clark
Monterey County Place Names; Donald T. Clark
Highway 17; Richard Beal
Georgiana: Feminist Reformer of the West;
    Georgiana B. Kirby
California Central Coast Railways; Rick Hamman
Steinbeck Country Narrow Guage: Fabing &Hamman
Late Harvest: Wine History of the Santa Cruz Mountains;
    Michael Holland
Santa Cruz is in the Heart; Geoffrey Dunn